This is a compilation of our thoughts and observations on our surroundings and encounters throughout our years in New York. Over time, we have been slowly digested, and the edges of our hesitation and European arrogance softened away, to be replaced by something American that we now treat as if it had always been part of us.

Although things on our side of the ocean have been looking dire for some time, it still seems to be the preferred land for the world's projections, if not its dreams.

We took this opportunity to create many new things, as well as rediscover and update some older sketches.

"Coming to America" is seemingly every immigrant's favorite movie. It has a scene in it that we love to point out to whoever wants to listen. It features Eddie Murphy's character's seminal sentence: "When you think of garbage, think of Hakeem." A beautiful attitude for a wealthy prince from Zamunda, or anyone else for that matter.

As immigrants ourselves, we tried to make this credo our own, to inject a certain pride into everything we do. New York turned out to be fertile ground for us.

Thank you, America, for these last 18 years, and for so much more.

<u>When you think of garbage, think of karlssonwilker.</u>

—Jan & Hjalti
New York, August 2018

EXCLAIMER: The edges of sheets of paper can be sharp and lead to paper cuts and bleeding. Neither the authors, nor the publishers, and/or the distributors, and/or the resellers can be held responsible in any court of law for any damages resulting from any physical interaction with these hereby presented printed sheets of paper.

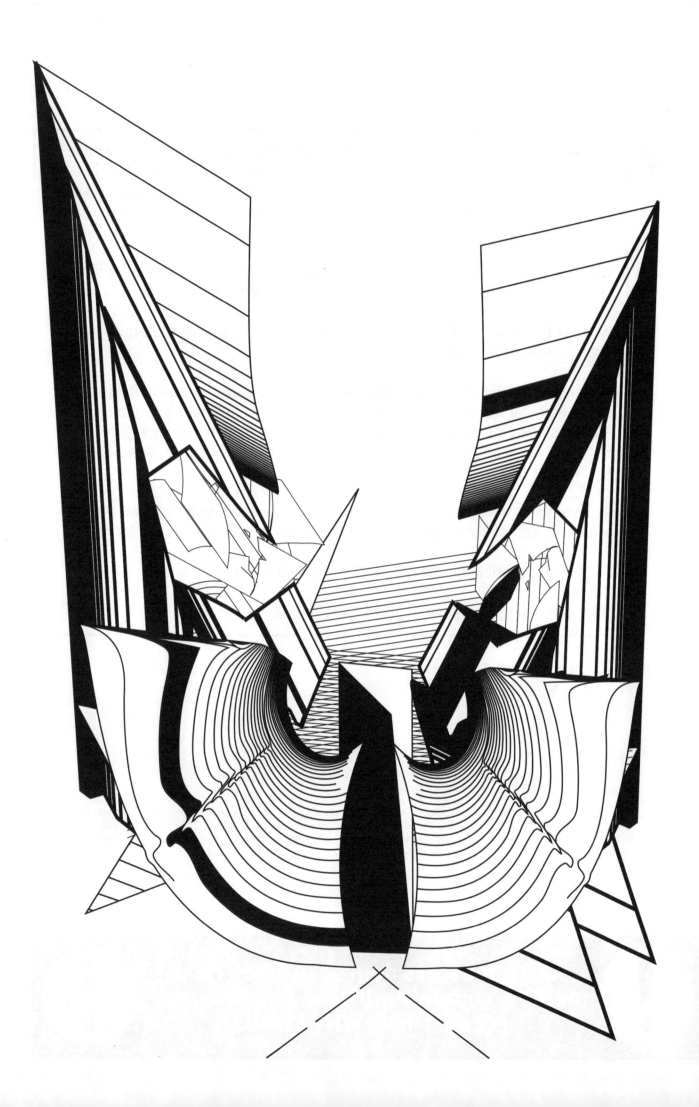

last night in ny:

TINY STORIES (8):

once, when i was very young, a stranger asked me into his car. he did not offer candy, but something about him led me to believe that he could be trusted. my mom said that i shouldn't ride with strangers. that's okay, he grumbled, she is probably just afraid that you will usurp her as the new prince of toy kingdom. what's that, i asked. you don't know about toy kingdom. sheesh. you are one dumb kid. then he drove off. when i asked my mom about toy kingdom, she just bowed her head and cried.

TINY STORIES (10):

i don't know if i have ever been as bored as when i sat in on dad's trial. i mean, the lawyers just kept talking and talking. occasionally they pointed at me. i figured this was the time when i was supposed to look pathetic, but i don't know if it came across right. i had to wear a suit and it was itchy. also, there was some old woman on the jury who kept looking at me like i was lunch. anyway, dad got off scott free and now i get to live with him. i'd be upset but he lets me drink and says i can screw girls if i want.

past performance does not guarantee future outcome

Prior to being cracked, the Liberty Bell became notorious as the highest pitched bell in its weight and size class.

WELCOME TO THE UNITED STATES

PLEASE CHECK / CIRCLE BELOW AND HAND OVER TO YOUR IMMIGRATION OFFICER:

[]   FAKE IT TILL YOU MAKE IT

[]   HARD WORK PAYS OFF

[]   OOOH, DOUBLE CHOCOLATE CHIP ICE CREAM!

google "the uncultured majority"

defendant: i didn't know the gun was loaded.

exhibit A: i didn't know the defendant was loaded.

hello america: superlatives are the worst!

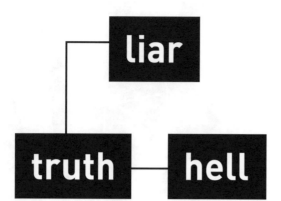

liar

truth   hell

WhiskeyTangoFoxtrott

< WTF, 2 dances?

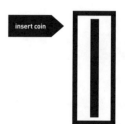

insert coin

the effect of drugs on designers:

the effect of drugs on breakfast:

the effect of religion on male perception:

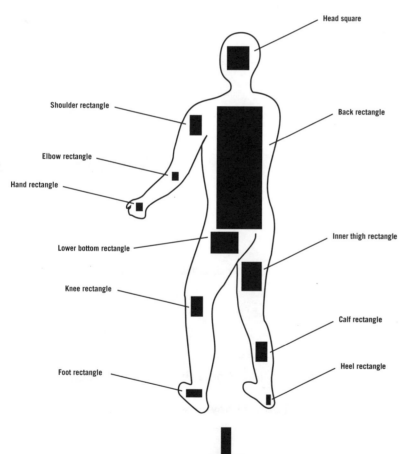

Head square

Shoulder rectangle

Back rectangle

Elbow rectangle

Hand rectangle

Lower bottom rectangle

Inner thigh rectangle

Knee rectangle

Calf rectangle

Foot rectangle

Heel rectangle

TINY STORIES (15):

one day i am going to fight like my old man. he killed a lot of people and that made him tough. i know that when we go out he is always aware of where the exits are and who is around him. once the waiter popped out of nowhere and my dad had him on the floor before you even knew what had happened. i tried to do the same thing to some kid at school, but i got my ass beat. when i told my dad he just shook his head and apologized for being such a bad influence. don't worry dad, i said, that sucker had it coming.

the effect of children on men:

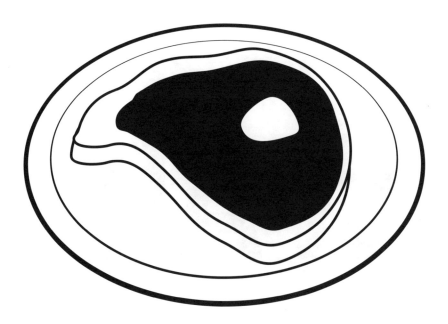

When I saw all these images of these starving kids in Syria, I just knew that
I had to react in a personal way, so I drew this grass-fed 16oz. steak for them.

WAR

WAR

complete the following sentence:

Little Johnny will _____ most of his classmates and teachers at school tomorrow.

large ice cube

childhood

$$\text{🛸} = \text{🍔}$$

$$\text{🛸} - \text{🍔} = 0$$

$$\text{🛸} + \text{🛸} = 2\text{🍔}$$

$$\text{🛸} + \text{🍔} = \text{USA}$$

AWESOME-R-US

CONSTITUTION-BASED FEDERAL REPUBLIC AND A STRONG DEMOCRATIC TRADITION SINCE 1776. RUGGED MOUNTAINS, VAST CENTRAL PLAINS, BROAD RIVER VALLEYS, AND HIGH-QUALITY SOUTH EAST ASIAN HEROIN. NATIVES TALK FROM A DISTANCE OF TWO FEET, ANY CLOSER IS VIEWED AS UNCOMFORTABLE. MOST PEOPLE THINK THERE ARE THREE TYPES OF PEOPLE: CITIZENS, TOURISTS, AND ILLEGALS. AND JEANS ARE EVERYWHERE.

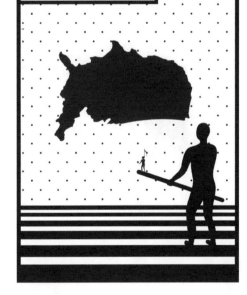

How things work (32):

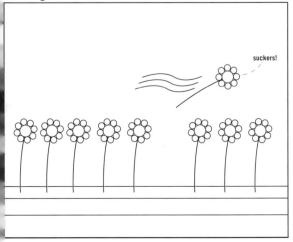

suckers!

The mice that live in the White House have been so secluded for hundreds of years that as of 2010 they are considered a different species.

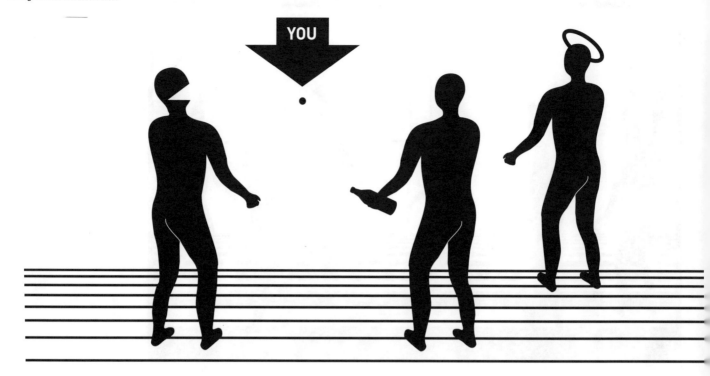

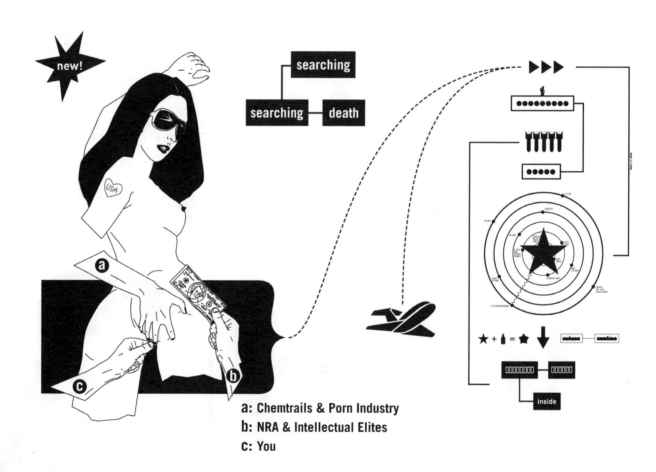

a: Chemtrails & Porn Industry
b: NRA & Intellectual Elites
c: You

UNFORTUNATELY MY FIRST WIFE I LOST TO DOMESTIC VIOLENCE

Everything is entertainment, IV (cooking):
Rabbit stew is ready

Everything is entertainment, XI (funeral):
Undertaker's blues

Everything is entertainment, XVII (
Back compliment

DJ Savespayze

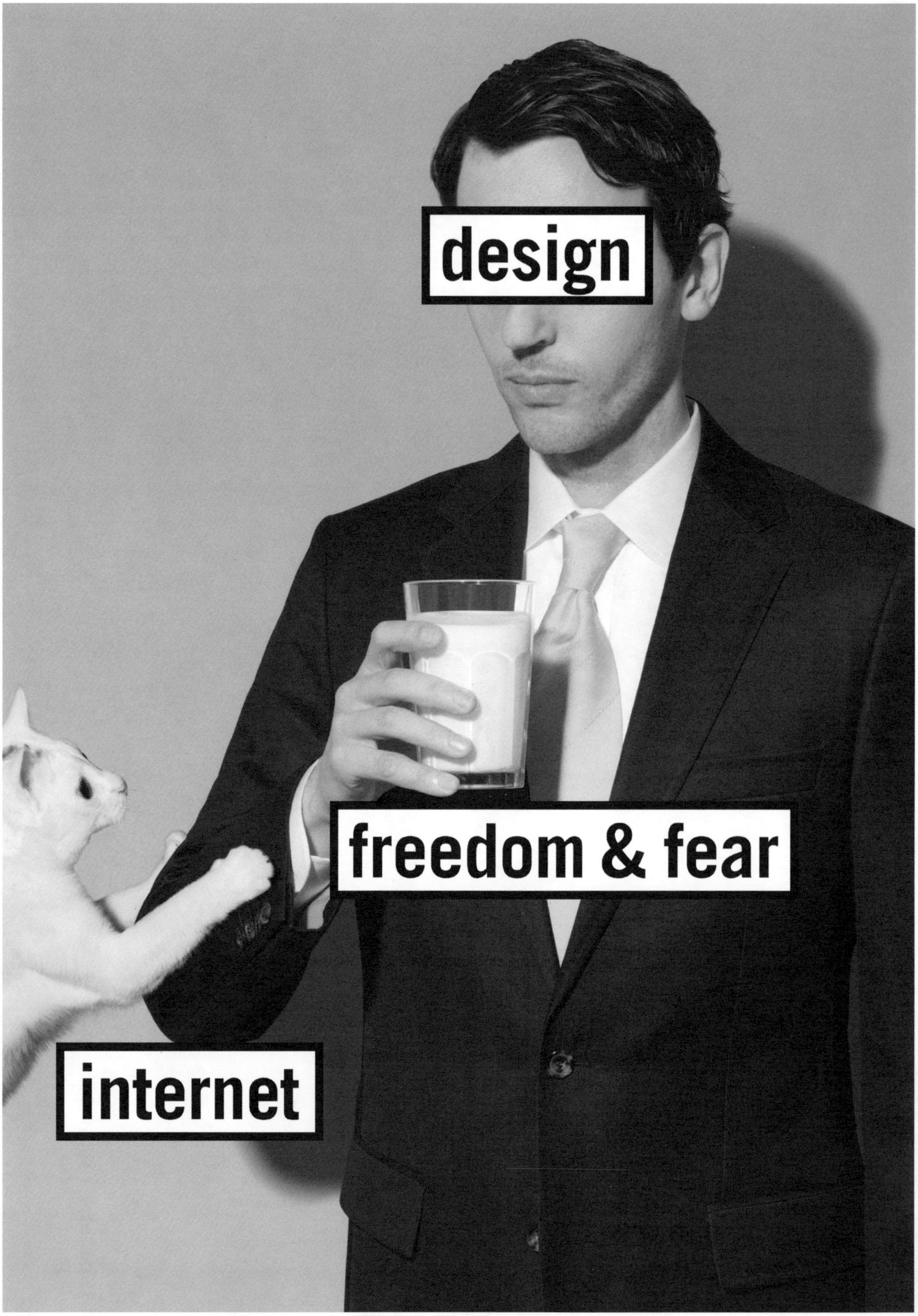
design
freedom & fear
internet

GILDED AGE, PERIOD OF GROSS MATERIALISM AND BLATANT POLITICAL CORRUPTION IN U.S. HISTORY DURING THE 1870S THAT GAVE RISE TO IMPORTANT NOVELS OF SOCIAL AND POLITICAL CRITICISM. THE PERIOD TAKES ITS NAME FROM THE EARLIEST OF THESE, THE GILDED AGE (1873), WRITTEN BY MARK TWAIN IN COLLABORATION WITH CHARLES DUDLEY WARNER. THE NOVEL GIVES A VIVID AND ACCURATE DESCRIPTION OF WASHINGTON, D.C., AND IS PEOPLED WITH CARICATURES OF MANY LEADING FIGURES OF THE DAY, INCLUDING GREEDY INDUSTRIALISTS AND CORRUPT POLITICIANS.
Encyclopædia Britannica

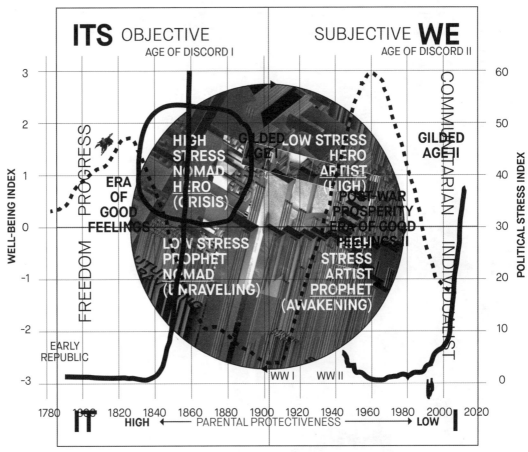

ITS OBJECTIVE
AGE OF DISCORD I

SUBJECTIVE WE
AGE OF DISCORD II

PROGRESS

COMMUNITARIAN

FREEDOM

INDIVIDUALIST

WELL-BEING INDEX

POLITICAL STRESS INDEX

ERA OF GOOD FEELINGS

HIGH STRESS NOMAD HERO (CRISIS)

GILDED AGE I

LOW STRESS HERO ARTIST (HIGH)

GILDED AGE II

POST-WAR PROSPERITY ERA OF GOOD FEELINGS II

LOW STRESS PROPHET NOMAD (UNRAVELING)

STRESS ARTIST PROPHET (AWAKENING)

EARLY REPUBLIC

WW I   WW II

IT

HIGH ← PARENTAL PROTECTIVENESS → LOW

I

3 2 1 0 -1 -2 -3

60 50 40 30 20 10 0

1780 1800 1820 1840 1860 1880 1900 1920 1940 1960 1980 2000 2020

 ERA OF GOOD FEELINGS, ALSO CALLED ERA OF GOOD FEELING, NATIONAL MOOD OF THE UNITED STATES FROM 1815 TO 1825, AS FIRST DESCRIBED BY THE BOSTON COLUMBIAN CENTINEL ON JULY 12, 1817. ALTHOUGH THE "ERA" GENERALLY IS CONSIDERED COEXTENSIVE WITH PRESIDENT JAMES MONROE'S TWO TERMS (1817–25), IT REALLY BEGAN IN 1815, WHEN FOR THE FIRST TIME, THANKS TO THE ENDING OF THE NAPOLEONIC WARS, AMERICAN CITIZENS COULD AFFORD TO PAY LESS ATTENTION TO EUROPEAN POLITICAL AND MILITARY AFFAIRS. THE PREDOMINANT ATTITUDE WAS WHAT IN THE 20TH CENTURY BECAME KNOWN AS ISOLATIONISM.
Encyclopædia Britannica

THE US of A

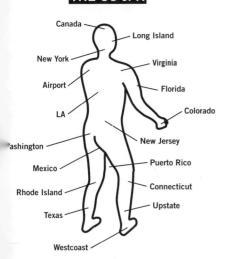

Canada
Long Island
New York
Virginia
Airport
Florida
LA
Colorado
Washington
New Jersey
Mexico
Puerto Rico
Rhode Island
Connecticut
Texas
Upstate
Westcoast

THIS IS NEW! THE UNBEATABLE CUSTOMER SERVICE:
WARM AND LOVING COLORFUL DESIGN!
IF THAT'S WHAT YOU'RE MISSING AND YOU START TO FREEZE AND YOU THINK TO YOURSELF: I DON'T LIKE THIS B/W-GRAPHIC-STUFF, THE WORLD ITSELF IS COLD ENOUGH...! JUST HAVE A LOOK AT THESE NICE LITTLE BUNNIES, PLAYING AND SITTING IN THE GARDEN OF HUMANITY. VIRGINITY IS THEIR BIG GOAL, BUT FOR HOW LONG...? AFTER SOME MINUTES OF STARING AT OUR LITTLE FRIENDS, SOON YOUR HEART WILL BE FULL OF WARMTH AND LOVE. AND IF YOU LOOK CLOSE ENOUGH, MAYBE SOME OF THESE GUYS WILL TWINKLE AND SMILE, SO THAT YOUR FACE WILL WEAR A GLANCE AND YOU WON'T CARE ANYMORE ABOUT STUFF LIKE WARM OR COLD GRAPHICS. CONGRATULATIONS!

initial TOC

TINY STORIES (12):

yesterday i ate at a new restaurant. i had heard that the clientele were a cut above the rest. like me. i was surprised to discover that the elite are every bit as tangible as the rest. the food was good, and the preparation impeccable. sometimes when i close my eyes i see lights and i can imagine myself as one great branch on the tree of life. when i open them again all i see is lobster bisque. these twerps here wouldn't know a good lobster bisque from a hole in the head.

Great Designers are made, not born.

The Better Design Video Series®

Over Four Million Sold!

2 FREE VIDEOS!
Advanced Oral Design Techniques, our free 30-minute video, is guaranteed to increase your design-making pleasure. Great Design 7 Days A Week shows you even more creative ways to ignite intense design excitement.

Interspersed with explanations and advice from nationally recognized design therapists, each video features explicit design scenes of everyday couples sharing their most intimate and passionate moments. Listen to what they say. Watch what they do. And then set off on your own design journey.

Western culture uses the thumbs-up to indicate a good job, used by World War II pilots to communicate that they were "good to go" with ground crews.

V or Victory hand was used during World War II to indicate a victory. During the Vietnam War, it was adopted by the counterculture in America as a symbol of peace.

The shaka sign or "hang loose", is a friendly gesture adopted by local Hawaiian culture and customs, and visiting surfers in the 1960s.

The raised fist is a symbol of defiance and resistance often associated with both left-wing politics and oppressed groups from the 1960s in America.

A fist bump or dap, originated among Black soldiers during the Vietnam War in 1969, as part of the Black Power Movement.

The devil horns or "rock on" was used as a Satanic salute during the 1960s, appearing in editions of the Satanic Bible.

Honorable Mentions: Air Quotes, "Talk to the Hand", Loser, Shooting Finger, High-Five

*Sources: Wikipedia, The Language Trainers, ABC News. Illustrations by: Freepik

For our readers' consideration:

Exercise 1

STOPPING THE STREAM

1. INHALE: As you get ready to urinate, inhale deeply.

2. EXHALE AND PUSH OUT: Exhale slowly and forcefully push out the urine. (Clenching your teeth will intensify the practice.)

3. INHALE AND CONTRACT YOUR PC: Inhale and contract your PC muscle to stop the flow of urine midstream.

4. EXHALE AND PUSH OUT AGAIN: Exhale and start urinating again.

5. REPEAT UNTIL FINISHED: Repeat steps 3 and 4 (urinating as you exhale and stopping the stream as you inhale) three to six times or until you have finished going to the bathroom.

EXERCISE 4

PC PULL-UPS

1. Inhale and concentrate on your prostate, perineum, and anus.

2. As you exhale, contract your PC muscle around your prostate and around your anus while at the same time contracting the muscles around your eyes and mouth.

3. Inhale and relax, releasing your PC, eye, and mouth muscles.

4. Repeat steps 2 and 3, contracting your muscles as you exhale and releasing them as you inhale, nine to thirty-six times.

Possible transformation of consciousness

Boundaries between you and partner dissolve

Pleasure pulses through entire body

Pleasure floods your brain

Pleasure expanding up your spine

Pleasure felt primarily in your genitals

Finish lovemaking with energy radiating through your body

Multiple whole-body orgasms

Draw energy up spine to brain using the Orgasmic Upward Draw

"Contractile phase" orgasm (involuntary PC contractions)

"Point of No Return" (ejaculation for men or single orgasm for women)

- Ordinary "Big Bang" ejaculatory orgasm for men or single orgasm for women
- Multiple whole-body orgasm with Orgasmic Upward Draw

Exercise 3

BECOMING A MULTI-ORGASMIC MAN

1. LUBRICATE: Start by lubricating your penis. (Lubrication, as you may already know, will increase your sensations and make it possible to solo cultivate longer. Oil is generally better than lotion, which dries up more quickly.)

2. SELF-PLEASURE: Self-pleasure however you like.

3. PAY ATTENTION TO YOUR AROUSAL: Pay close attention to your arousal rate. Once again, try to notice your increasing levels of arousal: notice the tingling at the root of your penis, notice the stages of erection, notice your breathing change and your heart rate increase.

4. BREATHE AND CONTRACT YOUR PC MUSCLE: As you feel yourself getting close to the point of no return, stop, breathe deeply, and lightly contract your PC muscle around your prostate. You can press on your penis or perineum, but your breath and your PC muscle are the most important, as is stopping in time.

5. FEEL ORGASMIC CONTRACTIONS IN YOUR PELVIS: Continue to pleasure yourself, coming increasingly close to the point of no return. If non-arousal is 0 and ejaculation is 10.0, then orgasm is at 9.8, so go slow. Start and stop, arousing yourself more and more (9.0, 9.1, and so on), and let yourself fall back into a contractile-phase orgasm without falling forward into an ejaculation. Notice the involuntary contraction of your prostate (and anus) that occurs during contractile-phase orgasm. Remember that these prostate orgasms may feel like mini-orgasms at first. Eventually they will be indistinguishable from ejaculatory orgasms, but you need to walk before you can run.

6. ENJOY: After you have peaked several times without ejaculating, stop. You will feel peaceful and/or energized afterward. You may even notice the sexual energy starting to rise in your body as tingling or prickling in your torso or head. This is completely natural and the beginning of transforming your genital orgasms into whole-body orgasms.

The Multi-Orgasmic Man, Mantak Chia & Douglas Abrams, ISBN 0062513362

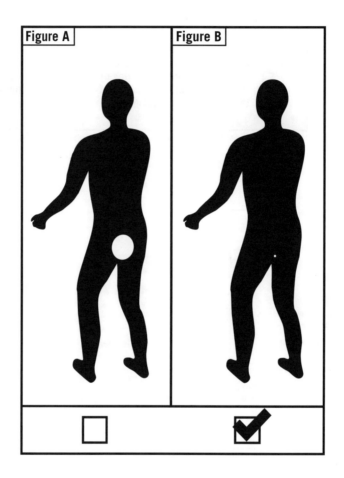

design

life & death

internet

When everything is on sale:

THE MORE YOU BUY, THE MORE YOU SAVE.

karlssonwilker on America

A conversation between Jan Wilker and Adrian Shaughnessy

The ambition for the following conversation (in fact, an exchange of emails) was to tease out some thinking about the current state of life—and work—in 21st century USA, and to investigate the challenges and realities of running a design studio in the city that never sleeps. Neither Wilker or Shaughnessy are American. But both bring a deep-rooted need to find an answer to the question, what makes America, America?

AS: Karlssonwilker on America. Now, there's a beguiling prospect. What angle will you take? Celebratory, critical, eulogistic? You are German, Jan. Hjalti your design partner is Icelandic, and your studio members come from all over the world. This gives you a wonderful vantage point from which to view the most powerful nation on earth. And yet, with America, an infinity of responses are possible. Everyone cultivates their own version of America. Although I'm a Brit, emotionally, I am American.

There are aspects of US life and culture that make me want to scream with rage (hello Donald! hello NRA!), and there are aspects that make me glad to be alive (the landscape, the art and culture, the great cities). I was born into the first generation of Brits who grew up with US TV shows, US pop music, and US style. I loved it all, and felt part of it. Jack Kerouac means more to me than Charles Dickens (and I love Dickens); Miles Davis means more to me than Edward Elgar. Jackson Pollock v Constable? No contest. I am shaped by American culture—both the high and the low versions. And that's why I feel entitled to say that I'm dismayed by so much that is happening in contemporary America.

It's more than the awfulness of the new president. Race relations, corporate greed, and mass shootings all make me despair about my beloved country. Am I right to feel this way? Is the country in terminal decline, or is the nation going through a sticky patch before emerging as a refreshed giant? As long ago as the 1970s, the British writer JG Ballard was able to say: "The American Dream has run out of gas. The car has stopped. It no longer supplies the world with its images, its dreams, its fantasies. No more. It's over. It supplies the world with its nightmares now: the Kennedy assassination, Watergate, Vietnam."

JW: Adrian, here's a non-response to your overwhelming start. I'll call it a cop-out assemblage, to downplay its incoherence. And, I'll be using this first reply as a warm-up. As you know, we initially thought about topics for this publication such as: "Karlssonwilker on arrogance"; "Karlssonwilker on friendliness"; "Karlssonwilker on neighborhood".

Eventually, we realized that these are all effortlessly embodied within the topic of "America". As for nearly everything, multiple angles are needed to make sense of something, and as universalists, and designers, this is all we can offer. We are pursuing an eclectic collection of thoughts and observations, recent or from many years ago, heavy or light, relevant or seemingly from a different era. This is a country we arrived in as guests. And we still are guests. Although our sense of outsiderness has weakened over the years, there should still be enough distance left for us to operate in.

About the despair you mention, the US movie character archetype—"former college quarterback/homecoming king", comes to mind. The one that didn't age well, and is stuck in past glories. Two storylines exist for this character. He's either the villain, past and current bully, or he is the tragic figure that only at the very end blossoms into strength. The base character, both villain or hero, is forced to share a pivotal moment when he (most likely a he, rather than a she), either loses forever or recalls his long forgotten power, showing it off one last time, surprising himself in the process, and fixing his alcoholism/marriage/earth/ team championship/universe, and becoming a somebody at last. And sometimes even the villain gets swept into the hero's final glow, ending his bullying days forever, as the radiance of belated resurrection/payback/resurgence/belief reaches through the screen right into the audience's lives, if only for a second.

It seems that this is where the USA finds itself right now. At a crossroads, at the pivotal moment. The United States is both the life-long bully and the tragic former small-town hero with slivers of past greatness, and soon to experience a final downfall or belated ascent to glory.

The New World, as the Old World used to call this place, turned out to disregard the rest of the world's hopes and dreams as a beacon for all, and became just another country. I'm ecstatic to see the ad banners of Chinese brands on display during sports events, or Chinese wayfinding around high-end US outlet shopping malls, reminding us of what has already been done to others, by the USA. The days are numbered for the former high-school star quarterback, no one wanting to wear his team jacket—and if he would only make his way to the local stadium, he would see the new generation of excellent quarterbacks.

As you can see, I'm inconsistent with my position towards America—I do as I please, the luxury and deception of a legal alien. Self-inflicted (arrogance/war) or through injury (life), our movie character's adolescent dreams stayed unfulfilled and bitterness moved in. He died on the college football field/any other school/university/sports/music/important-at-that-time event, yet all he needs today is a tiny nudge to get him back to life.

AS: I think your "inconsistency" is entirely rational. America is too vast and too complex to allow anyone to have a single unwavering position. You mention two things, both of which prompted me to think about two experiences I had in the past year that affected my thinking about America. The first is your reference to Chinese banners at sporting events and Chinese language wayfinding in shopping malls. The second is your reference to war and American arrogance. The two experiences these brought to mind were, firstly, a trip to China that I undertook last summer, and secondly, watching the utterly captivating documentary by Ken Burns and Lynn Novick—The Vietnam War.

Let's deal with China first. I spent three weeks in the country at the invitation of a Chinese art and design institution that prepares students for study in the West. During my time there I visited five cities—Beijing, Shanghai, Guangzhou, Shenzhen and Chengdu. Each city was a revelation. China has embarked on a program of urbanization that dwarfs all other attempts to build the metropolises of the future.

This explosion of architecture and urban infrastructure made me compare it to the only other superpower on the planet—America. When I first went to the USA (in the nineties) I was joyously overwhelmed by the scale of the great cities. To my British eyes, they seemed to represent an almost supra-human achievement. But when I go back now, I get a sense of decline and regression. Nowhere is this more apparent than on the New York subway. It's like a crumbling mansion, sinking into itself. Contrast this with China's gleaming subways, bullet trains and futuristic railway stations, and America looks off the pace. Your phrase— "soon to experience a final downfall" aptly sums up my feeling about American infrastructure.

This feeling of decline (or more accurately, a feeling of not learning from past mistakes) was reinforced by watching the compelling documentary The Vietnam War. Time and again, acts of staggering political mendacity were revealed. In fact, it is not an exaggeration to conclude that the horror of Vietnam was both unnecessary in the first place, and disastrously prolonged—resulting in the deaths of millions of Vietnamese and Americans—for one reason and one reason alone: The monumental vanity of America's rulers.

The public were repeatedly lied to, and the death toll soared as successive American administrations, firstly under Kennedy, then Johnson, and finally Nixon sought to save face. The documentary struggled to find anyone who could defend America's conduct in Vietnam. Even hardened vets who had gone willingly to fight for their country, returned disillusioned. Many—though not all—came back as pacifists and antiwar supporters. Anyone watching all 13 episodes was left with a feeling of despair. This despair is all the worse for those of us who love America.

As I said at the beginning of this conversation, I think of myself as emotionally a US citizen. I am a product of US mid-century liberal values. And despite everything—and by everything I mean Trump, the NRA, and the alt-right—I'm still in love with the country, and I'll never lose the excitement of arriving in Manhattan for the first time and instantly plugging into the cultural matrix that I had admired from afar for so long.

But unlike you, I went back home after my first visit. You stayed. Why? And what keeps you there?

JW: I'll start by describing my first 24 hours in the US, which was in the summer of 1999, and went as follows: I arrived at JFK. I was traveling light with only a tennis bag, and I was ready for my three month internship. All I had was an address in Brooklyn of the typical "friend-of-a-friend" who would allow me to stay for two nights. Once in front of his building, I discovered that there was no one there to let me in. Dragging my little bag behind me, I took a quick trip to Manhattan to see what it was like. Then I returned and sat for six hours outside a deli at the corner, with the entrance in sight.

The friend-of-a-friend didn't show up that day, or the next day, or the next night. Later I learned that he was in the hospital with his girlfriend giving birth to their child. Outside the deli a conversation soon started with some of the deli regulars sitting in the late sun on little wooden crates. This put my very rudimentary English to the test. In the following hours I must have used an endless combination of 15 words, making up very short, incomplete sentences. One of the old men, a Vietnam vet, asked me at some point long after sunset if I wanted to stay with him that night. I had no plan other than to keep sitting there waiting, so I ended

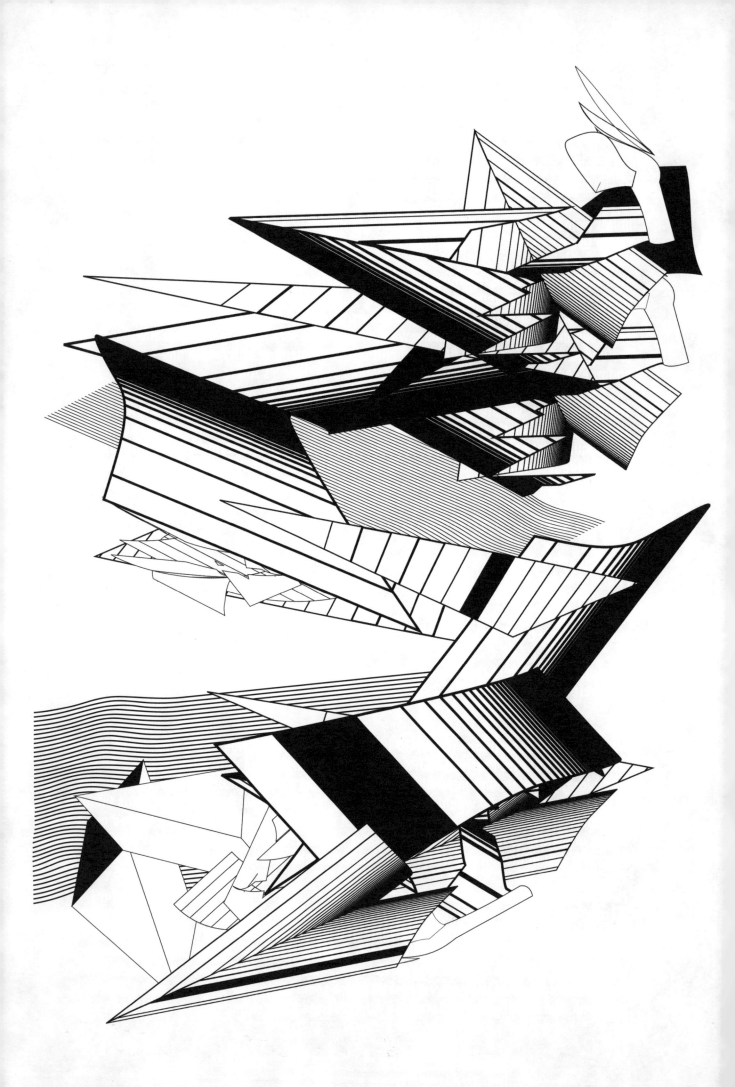

up in his tiny, very rundown basement apartment few blocks away, where he offered me his bed. Roaches scattered everywhere when I opened the sheets. Hundreds all over the room. He stayed on his sofa. He was the first Vietnam vet I had ever seen in real life. Back in Germany I had heard and seen movies about them and their war. His hands were constantly shaking and he mumbled in his sleep. I felt good and safe while I was there, and I slept deeply and soundly. I was very tired. I bought him breakfast the next morning. He paraded me around his neighborhood and introduced me as his new friend from Germany. I ended up staying with him one more night, before I found the friend-of-a-friend back at his home. I do not remember the name of the Vietnam vet, nor the exact address.

To your question about staying in the US: It was never my dream to live in New York, or in America, for that matter. I grew up in Ulm, a city in southern Germany, back when it had some of the largest US military bases. You would see GIs around the city, and we already had a Burger King when most other cities had only just gotten their first McDonalds. We would see them drive around in their extra-wide Humvees, wearing baseball hats with skilfully folded shields, throwing and catching balls with leather gloves, and overall looking otherworldly and super cool.

I did have a stars and stripes flag in my room. But at no time did I see myself living in the US. I think I would have been happy in Stuttgart, or in Berlin, or anywhere else for that matter. At that time I had nothing better to do, and it felt right. I think it was the same for Hjalti. Stefan [Sagmeister] announced his sabbatical and we needed to come up with something to do. Hjalti had worked with Stefan for four years, and I was the intern. Hjalti and I could only gain from trying to start a studio together. Initially, the challenge to work in a city with so many excellent designers was exhilarating and positively challenging, but we quickly ended up in our little bubble. Without post-rationalizing too much, we turned inwards quite quickly and concentrated mostly on our selves, our little kingdom. Nearly everything else back then was boring, repetitive, and corporate, at least in our youthful heads and hearts.

Over time there are two things I came to appreciate about New York. One is that being here calmed me down. While the city might be frantic and demanding, the longing to live in one of the world's major cities is already fulfilled, which is where a certain calmness comes from. With it, I could focus on expending my energy to push forward, commit to being here, working and designing. Without inner restlessness, things become simpler. The second thing is being able, after a trip abroad, to keep on exploring that country's, or a region's culture through food, people, events, or even classes seamlessly here in New York. This is made possible, of course, by the large expat groups here. Connected to this is that many people visit New York, so friendships from around the world are possible. I don't know if I made myself clear here. I will re-read Kafka's Amerika now.

AS: I completely get the idea that the frenetic pace and ceaseless energy of New York is an incentive for you to do great work. I felt the same when I moved to London as a young wannabe designer. I think it's what mega-cities do. They take a blow torch to your emotions. And it's certainly what I felt on my first visit to NYC. I loved the fact that you could find diners open at 2.00am, and go to Tower Records at midnight. On my first night I was woken at 3.00am by the dust carts emptying dumpsters in the alley beside my hotel. The roar of traffic and police sirens lasted all night, and people started shouting early in the morning. Breakfast TV pumped caffeinated colour into my retinas. None of this was conducive to complacency or inertia. It was a signal to do something.

But this conversation is not just about NYC, it's about America, in all its immensity. Yet any attempt to encapsulate the American nation in tidy aphorisms is doomed to fail. In fact, I learned an important lesson about relying on long-established prejudices and assumptions on a recent trip to Texas. I went to Austin—the State capital—and despite the abundance of cowboy boots, stetsons, and the signs in cafes saying "No Open Carry" (especially chilling to a gun-fearing Brit like me), Austin proved remarkably unlike the stereotypical impression of Texas I was clinging to. As someone said to me—you are in Austin, not in Texas. I think I know what he meant.

This experience made me question where my "understanding" of America comes from. I can't say I've traveled extensively in the USA. I've been to California, the North West, the South West, Chicago, New York, and a couple of Southern states, but I can hardly claim a deep familiarity with the place. And yet I feel I know America. Where does this come from? Well, it comes from literature, TV, and music, but mostly it comes from cinema.

You can argue that the essence of a nation is exhibited through its art. But I'd say that no nation has revealed itself on a more gargantuan scale than America has through its cinema. The USA can claim this because it was one of the first nations to have an indigenous movie industry and film culture. Other nations can make similar claims—France, Germany, Japan. But none can claim to have done it on a scale that compares to American cinema.

Ever since I learned to sit in front of a movie screen, I've been colonised by the aesthetics of American cinema. My understanding of American psychology, landscape, culture and idioms comes from America cinema. However, I'm not an uncritical viewer. I'm aware that as well as exhibiting the best side of America, movies also exhibit the worst: I'll mention the depiction of native Americans in Westerns, as a glaringly obvious example. I could add race hatred and the worshipping of guns as two other toxic elements. But you only know a nation by seeing all its faces and American cinema does this wonderfully.

This leads me to mention a concept that seems relevant to many American movies—the notion that America is first amongst all nations. Some call this the doctrine of American Exceptionalism. Wikipedia tells me that the term was actually coined by Joseph Stalin as a "critique of a revisionist faction of American Communists who argued that the American political climate was unique, making it an 'exception' to certain elements of Marxist theory". More recently, Ronald Reagan is credited as a leading proponent of this idea in the 20th century. And it's not hard to see that Trump and his supporters embrace the notion in a new and vehement way.

What about you? Does American Exceptionalism exist for you, or is it a national myth? And I suppose another related question—could you do what you do with karlssonwilker anywhere else in the world?

JW: If societies have a certain bandwidth, America focuses theirs heavily on the present and the immediate future. In contrast to that, Germany seems to focus on the past and the present, with the "future" regraded as a more abstract concept than one's own immediately upcoming experience. And I would guess that American Exceptionalism happened to be true at one point, gifted by late colonization, therefore late extraction, with slavery readily available, and early capitalism (and with no reparations in sight). For me, America has entered a post-exceptionalist phase, its confidence being kept alive by a populace that has no alternative model available, blinded by a past it doesn't quite care for anyway, and an imagined greatness, which might just be as strong as real greatness. What is left is exceptional obliviousness.

Side note to America's lack of interest in history: Its place seems to have been taken by a fanatical fascination with the Civil War, and the First and Second World Wars. On the one hand, this seems rightfully detail-oriented and real, and on the other, abstract and distant, like Star Wars fans, more of a hobby, and hopelessly incompatible with the real world. Studying wars as fan fiction means there is no learning from the past to be applied to the real world.

Warfare and entertainment are America's only true crafts. Unsurprisingly, both of them are frowned upon in Europe. All this leads to graphic design being approached and used as a form of entertainment, which is how it is practiced here. Entertainment in its purest, most positive form is noble and good-tempered, with a little under-the-belt quip here and there. Graphic designers in America are entertainers. This seems quite a departure from the systematic, logical approach found in Germany. You can see it at design conferences: European speakers are often too convoluted, too stiff, too boring, to get their points across. They can't tell a good story. They can't entertain. So I do not know of any place in the world, other than New York, where we could have gone this far with what we do. And what we are doing is largely dictated by our clients, with most of them in New York.

I should point out that I left Germany almost 20 years ago, therefore I'm comparing 90s Germany to today's America. My hope is that this vantage point can only heighten the subtle differences at play today. And when I refer to Germany, I sometimes dared myself to write "Europe". But I didn't.

The ability to be excited should in part stem from a disregard of history. For a graphic designer in the States, this means that it is up to the practitioner to deliver original or derivative work, as there are no inherent bonus points for either, no outside acknowledgment beyond what seems to work in the here-and-now. "Excitedness" is a powerful force and an important ally for the designer. It is beautiful and intoxicating to work in a country filled with people that are excitable. It's the start-up capital of the world! Intellectual approaches to work are boiled down to interesting bits for storytelling, for novelty. Within the tightness of commercialism, this is where space opens up for experimentation. Is Berlin or New York more open to experimentation? By any usually-employed parameters, it should be Berlin. But it might corrupt itself, stand in its own way, and discuss itself to death, allowing the fast-paced, anti-intellectual, entertainment-oriented New York to power ahead.

A systematic design approach, longing for understanding and respect, seems futile. Decisions are made within the entertainment scale, not on sustainability, longevity, or intellectual grounds. Intellectual rigor is detrimental here. It stands against the quickness of events. Who wants to propose a five-year roll-out design system to a headless chicken? The beauty of working here is exactly that: Designing for, as, and with headless chickens. Fast and action-packed, fearless, picking up bits and pieces, a different kind of life, enjoyment, and work.

To the question could I work in any place other than America, or New York in particular, I'd have to say, no. The reasons are obvious: An easy to learn language; everyone is an outsider/newcomer/expat/immigrant; no old local clans that control the flow of work; a city that attracts energetic people who want to get things done. And also, a design scene that is open, friendly, welcoming, helpful and kind, without needless competitiveness or a bunker mentality.

What helped us in the beginning was to be located in New York City. And it has changed quite a bit since we started. Most of the world had (and mostly still has) this romantic notion of this grand old dame of mega cities. Things and dreams are being projected onto you, and you gladly take it. America in the early 2000s gave us lot to rub against, grow with, agree with, and discuss. It gave us direction, allowing us to embrace it while keeping some of our rigidity.

AS: You have floated a ton of ideas that I'd like to follow up. I'm especially interested in the notion of "design as entertainment". And I'd like to challenge you on the notion that European speakers at design conferences can be boring. Yes, they can, and often are. But I've also sat through some staggeringly egotistical presentations by American speakers— speakers where the notion of self-criticality was an unknown phenomenon. Having said that, I once had to follow Aaron Draplin at an AIGA Conference in Chicago. He was pure energy and entertainment. I felt like a firework that had failed to ignite. He used Bob Seger as his on-stage entrance music. Now that's what I call entertainment.

But space and time (them again!) are against us. So, I'll bring this enjoyable "conversation" to a close by asking you to talk specifically about karlssonwilker—how does it work, who do you work with, and what are the principle challenges that you encounter?

JW: These days, Hjalti concentrates a bit more on new business development, while I run the projects, together with Sandra Shizuka, our associate partner and art director, who's been with us for almost eight years. We are also very glad to have designer Connor Muething with us, and Peter Saluk, who is our office manager. Our current intern is Nick Sheeran. We do not work with design freelancers, as their agency habits make them impossible to work with, specifically short-term. So it's just six people. We're a tight-knit team.

The vast majority of our projects are from one-time clients, for one-off projects. This has to do with the landscape here in America, where most of our clients are based, and where there's little interest in design studio monogamy. Who wants to settle down with one studio when so many different options and offerings are available? And it also has to do with the kind of client our studio attracts. In our now 18-year history, we only had one long-term client, with a continuous working relationship for seven years. So there's very little repeat business, and therefore almost no opportunity to synergize and to establish efficiency loops and repeatable processes. That's freedom. For the client, and for us. And the more freedom we have, the less safety we have. While this way of running a business is quite inefficient, restless, and often draining, it's what we know, and what we've gotten used to. And it's also exciting and continuously challenging. Projects vary from a few weeks to three, four years.

For me, American design is first and foremost about freedom. And although American design has a tendency to be quite naive at times, as many European, or European-centric, designers are quick to point out—what they usually miss is that it also means that you're allowed to fly.

After 16 years in the heart of Manhattan, right above a Dunkin' Donuts on 6th Avenue and 14th Street, we moved out to Ridgewood, Queens, into our own little building, with the studio on the ground floor, a large open glass storefront and a south-facing backyard garden, and me living directly above on the second floor. We were very lucky to have gotten the building, and we are in midst of setting up a little store and coffee window in the front. It's a welcome change and we're all embracing it. ¶

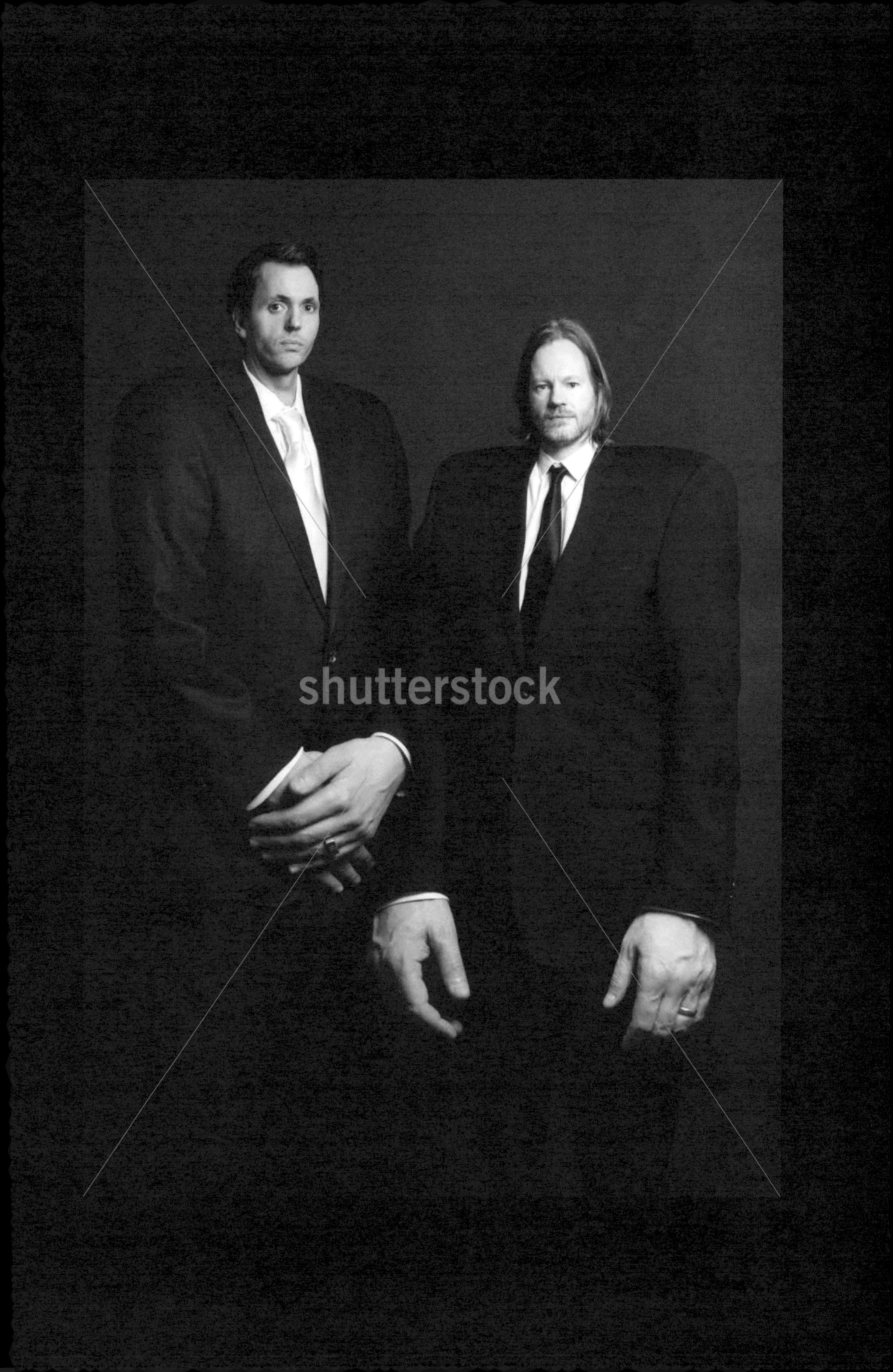

WELCOME TO RIDGEWOOD

Ridgewood is a quiet neighborhood in Queens, NY. It is 1.8 square miles in area.

Queens is 108 square miles in area, the largest of the boroughs.

39% of Queens is water.

Peter walks seven hours to work.

Hjalti (still) lives in Manhattan, which is 1.5 hours away by scooter.

★ karlssonwilker inc. ★
682 Woodward Avenue
Ridgewood, NY
US of A

- Old neighborhood
- New neighborhood

thefts   assaults   burglaries   robberies

Woodward Ave

GOTTSCHEER

LEFT FIELD

Neighborhood lessons and words:

"Bro this place has a mean bacon egg and cheese on a potato dill bun, OMG. that chedder cheese kills it. I never stay but they are always so nice, the atmosphere is so pleasent I really like it here."

In the beginning Ridgewood was mostly knitting mills and breweries. At one point there was also a textile factory. Every member of the Italian family living next door was diagnosed with cancer.

Tommy Ramone died up the street and around the corner from the Italian family (not from cancer or at the same time).

Our neighbors to the left still have the original speakeasy bar from Prohibition times in their basement.

From a recent article:

"Doors and windows open to the street? This could never happen in Manhattan, where even small office buildings have security cameras and a lobby desk where ID badges are issued to visitors. Yes, this must be the new home of karlssonwilker inc."

TOPOS

SUPER POLLO

JULIA'S

GWENDOLYN'S

Jan lives 20 steps away vertically.

Sandra lives within walking distance, theoretically.

Connor lives 8 minutes away by horse.

Nick lives 31 minutes away by heelies.

NORMA'S CORNER SHOPP

MORSCHER'S PORK STORE

Review of the week:

After today's visit to the store I was disappointed with the service and fraud. I wanted to buy the meat for the tatara, the expedition chose the meat of the worst species, instead of him grinded the ready to change the meat trying to me to necktie. It is what I wanted...a piece of "my" lying in the display cabinet next to the finished ground meat. So it does not matter where it is the meat on the raw tatara.

Six blocks down our street, a sign greets you. Tischlein deck' Dich,
it says, from a German fairy tale by the Brothers Grimm, translating to
"table-be-set"—announcing the local butcher shop's plenties. The first
time I walked in, the original butcher's son himself, already an old man
now, told me, in our shared mother tongue, that his mom, as well as
his mom's mother, could still remember when the Hindenburg flew over
this very neighborhood and the Germans could be found on their roofs
waving their perfectly pressed handkerchiefs towards the sky.
And further, a friend of his does roofing. When the roofs leak, another
layer of tar sheets go on top, about every 20 years or so. Over time,
the multiple layers get too heavy and they have to be peeled off before
they can fix the roof again. Sometimes, layer after layer, the butcher's
son's roofing friend gets all the way back to the late 1930s, early 40s.
That's when he would sometimes find large swastikas painted onto
some roofs, spanning the whole width of the building.
Since our building was built by Germans in 1930, at night I sometimes
imagine a very low hum emanating from a hidden hakenkreuz hovering
right above my head, in patient hibernation...

The White House has been
painted 657 times since it was
originally built which has
expanded its exterior walls 3"
in all directions.

DON'T GET
PLAYED
BY THE
GAME

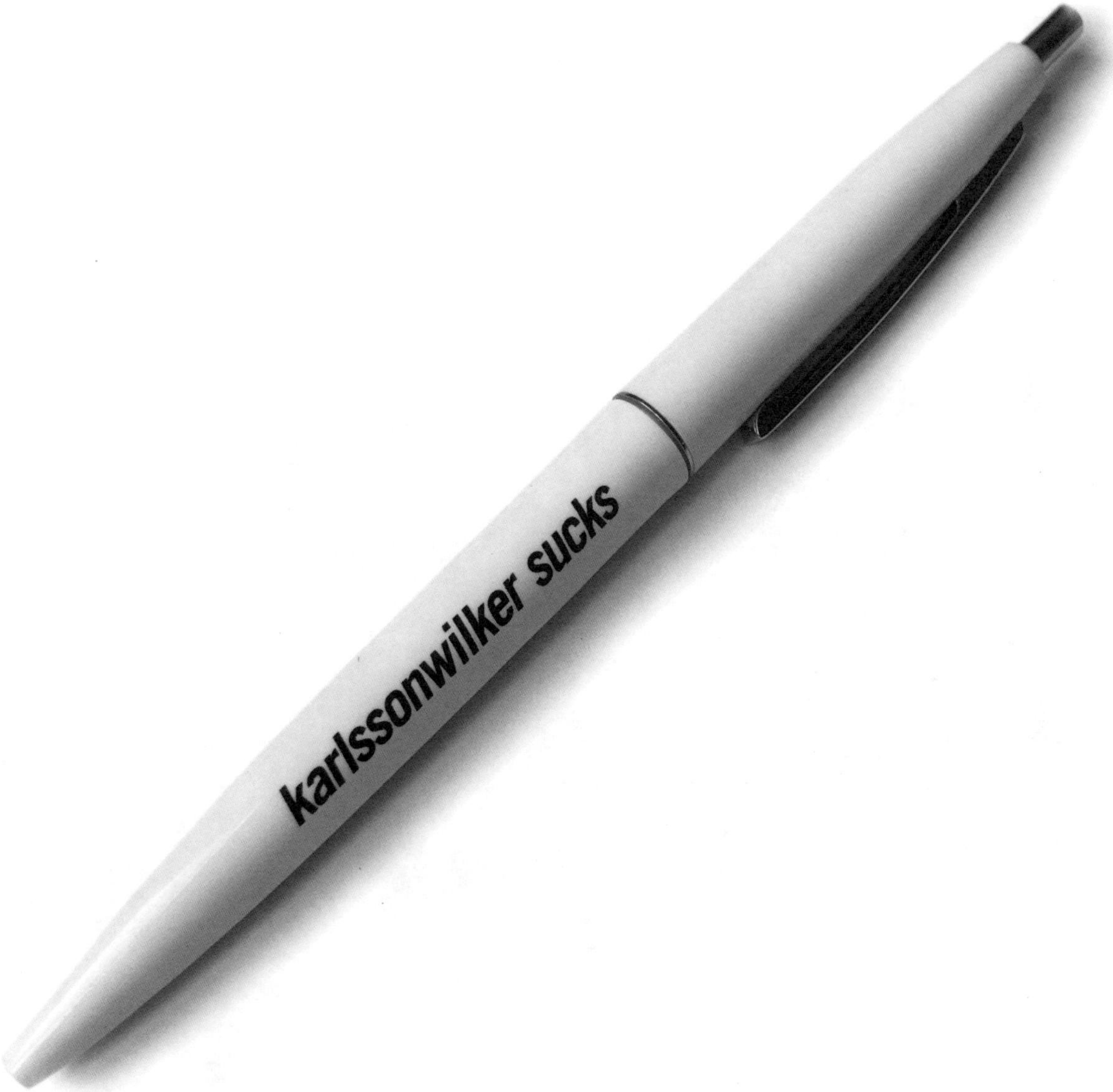
karlssonwilker sucks

ONE IN FOUR IMMIGRANTS

WILL BE DEPORTED. KARLSSONWILKER IS NOT HIRING.

KARLSSON

WILKER

< Wet Bald Eagle

GROWING OLD GRACEFULLY:

⬇⬇

DAYS BECOME WEEKS BECOME MONTHS BECOME YEARS BECOME LIVES BECOME MILLENNIA. AND WHILE IT'S NOT EASY DYING, NOW OR EVER, READING ABOUT IT HERE RIGHT NOW PUTS YOU ON A PATH TO PERSONAL GROWTH. DISCUSS.

Bald eagles are adapting their hunting method; in recent years, they have been sighted squashing their prey at high speeds. This change has resulted in a loss of talon sharpness over the past decade.

NEW OFFICES
NEW WEBSITE

OLD PROBLEMS

CALL 1-800 KARLSSONWILKER.COM

...el studio de los design sophistiqué y expertes!

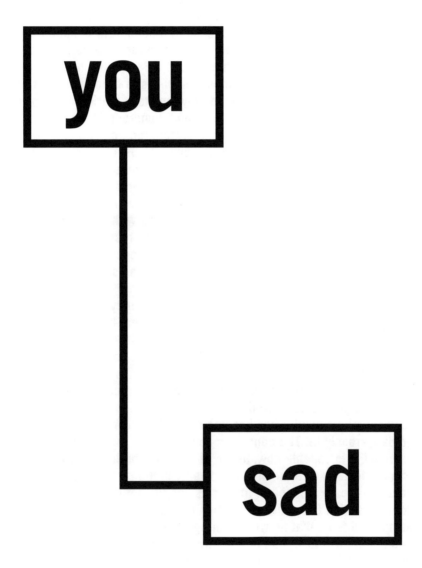

*Source: The 45th president of the United States of America

BOOK CLUB!

Excerpt from Little Golden America—Two Famous Soviet Humorists Survey These United States, by Ilya Ilf & Eugene Petrof, 1936:

..."America is rich. But it is not merely rich. It is phenomenally rich. It has everything—oil, grain, coal, gold, cotton—everything that can only lie beneath the earth or grow upon the earth. It has people—the best workers in the world—capable, neat, efficient, honest, hard-working. America marched toward its enrichment at a quick rate of speed. The country reminds one of a man who has made a rapid career, who at first sells suspenders from a push-cart on the East Side, then opens his own store of ready-made clothes and moves to Brooklyn. Then he opens a department store, begins to play the stock market and moves to the Bronx. And finally he buys a railroad, hundreds of steamships, two motion-picture factories, builds a skyscraper, opens a bank, joins a golf club, and moves to Park Avenue. He is a billionaire. He had striven for that goal all his life. He bought and sold everything in any old way. He dispossessed people, speculated, sat at the stock exchange from morning until night, he toiled sixteen hours a day, he awoke with the thought of money, he fell asleep with the same thought, and now he is monstrously wealthy. Now he may rest. He has villas by the ocean, he has yachts and castles, but he becomes ill with an incurable disease. He is dying, and no billions can save him.

The stimulus of American life has been and is money. Contemporary American technique grew up and developed so that money might be made faster. Everything that brings in money develops, and everything that does not bring money degenerates and wilts away. Gas, electricity, construction, and automobile companies, in their chase for money, have created a high standard of living. America has raised itself to a high degree of welfare, having left Europe far behind. But precisely at this point it has become clear that America is seriously and dangerously ill. The country is now facing its own reductio ad absurdum. It is capable now, today, of feeding a billion people, and yet it cannot feed its own hundred and twenty millions. It has everything needed to create a peaceful life for its people, yet it has come to such a pass that the entire population is in a state of unrest: the unemployed fears that he will never again find a job; the employed fears that he will lose his job; the farmer fears a crop failure, because then prices will increase and it will cost him more to buy bread, but he also fears a good crop, because then prices will fall and he will have to sell his produce for a pittance. The rich fear that bandits will kidnap their children, bandits fear that they will be placed in the electric chair. Immigrants fear that they will be deported from America; Negroes fear that they will be lynched; politicians fear elections; the average man fears illness, because then doctors will take everything he owns; the merchant fears that racketeers will come and riddle his store counters with a machine-gun fusillade."...

The copper used for the Statue of Liberty is so soft that each year the monument's breasts sag around 2".

This photo story is a satire and is not intended maliciously. karlssonwilker has invented all names, logos, and branding on the subject's clothing, except in cases when the public figure is being satirized. Any other use of real names is accidental and coincidental, or used as a fictional depiction or personality parody (permitted under Hustler Magazine v. Fallwell, 485 US 46, 108 S.Ct 876, 99 L.Ed.2d41 (1988)).

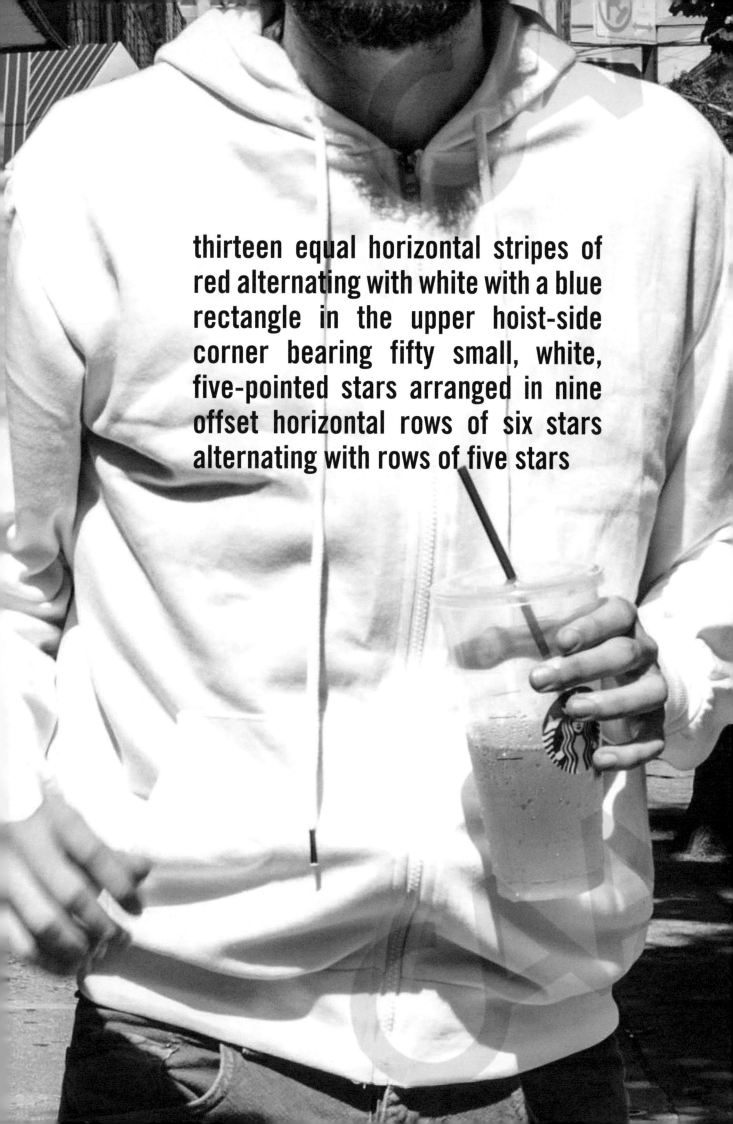

thirteen equal horizontal stripes of red alternating with white with a blue rectangle in the upper hoist-side corner bearing fifty small, white, five-pointed stars arranged in nine offset horizontal rows of six stars alternating with rows of five stars

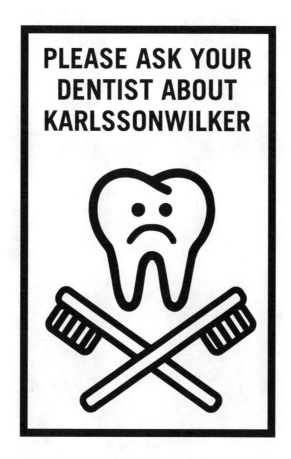

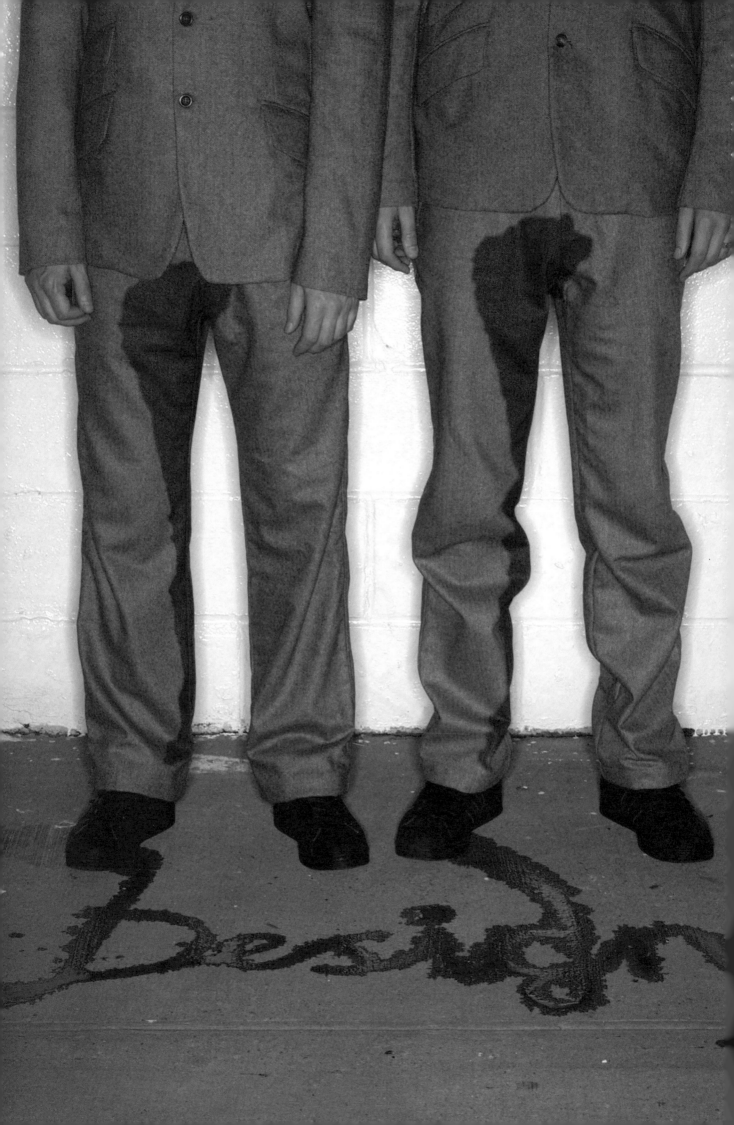